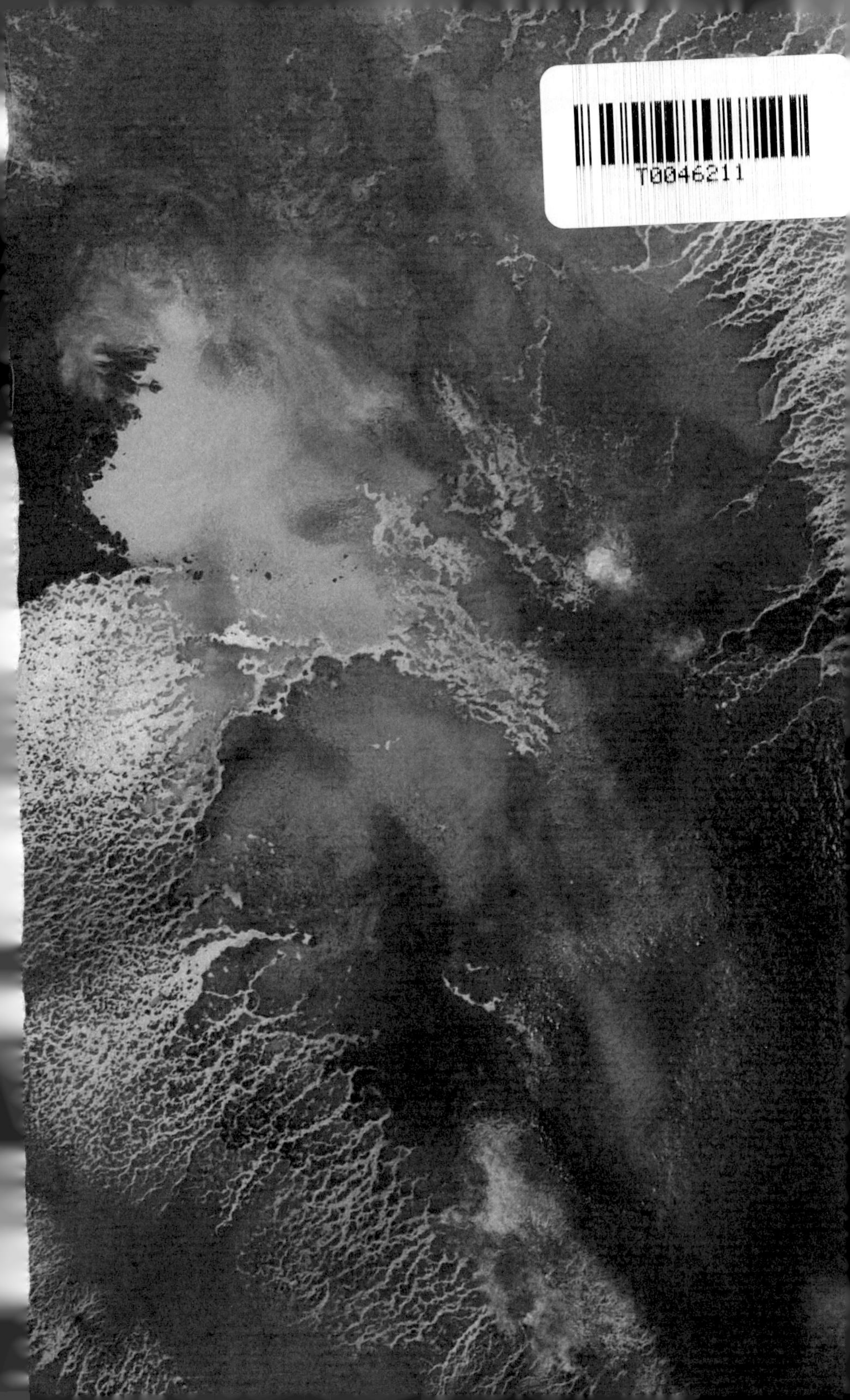
T0046211

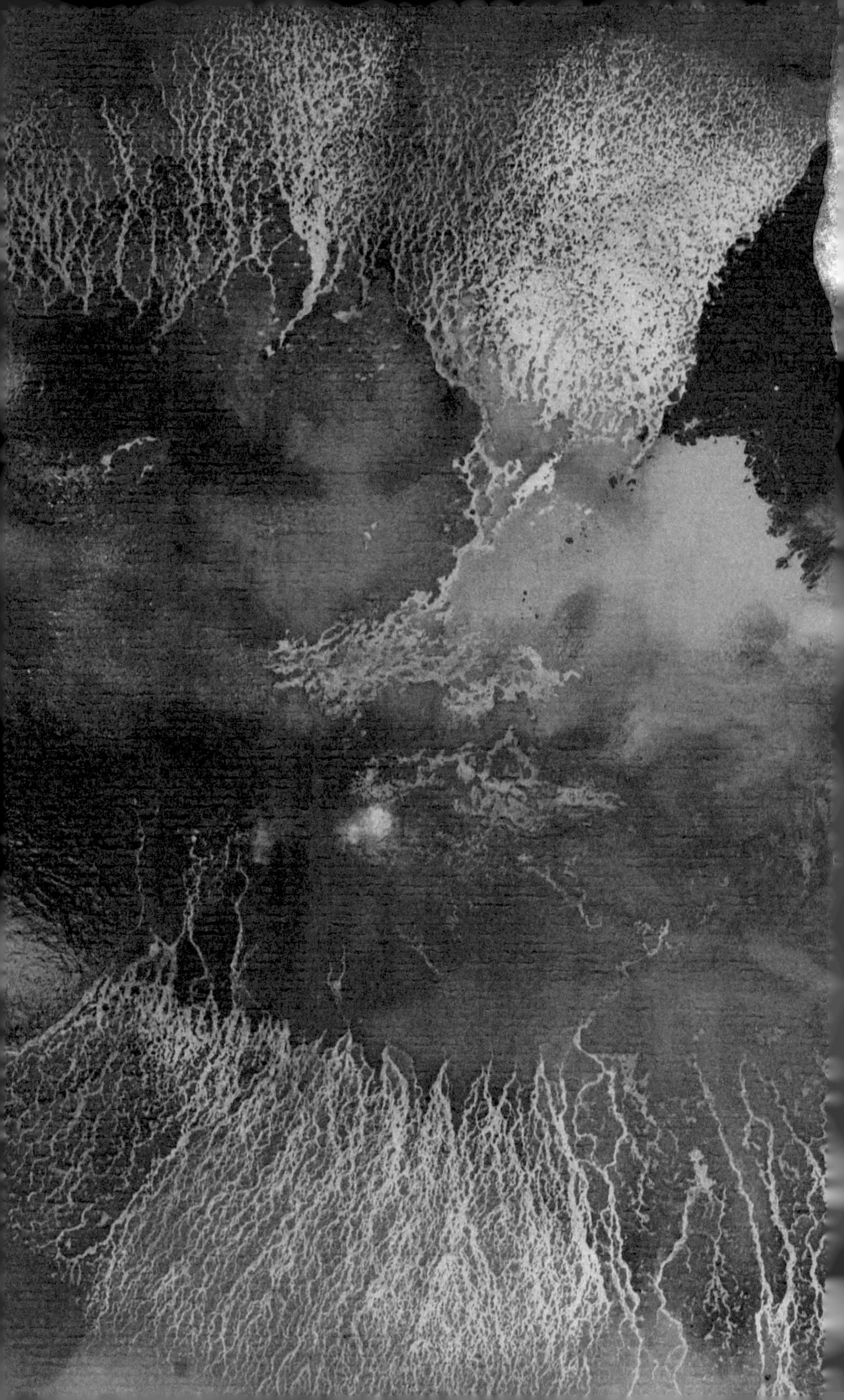

WET

DREAM

ERIN

ROBINSONG

Library and Archives Canada Cataloguing in Publication

Title: Wet dream / Erin Robinsong.
Names: Robinsong, Erin, author.
Description: Poems.
Identifiers: Canadiana (print) 20220246653 | Canadiana (ebook) 20220246793
ISBN 9781771315876 (softcover) | ISBN 9781771315883 (HTML) | ISBN 9781771315890 (PDF)
Classification: LCC PS8635.O266 W48 2022 | DDC C811/.6—dc23

Third Printing, 2023

We gratefully acknowledge the Canada Council for the Arts, the Government of Canada through the Canada Book Fund, and the Ontario Arts Council for their support of our publishing program.

Edited by Sonnet L'Abbé.
Cover image (indigo and rainwater ink) and endpapers (oak gall and iron water ink; copper pipe, sea salt, and vinegar ink; indigo and rainwater ink) by Flora Wallace.
Author photo by Andréa de Keijzer.

Design by LOKI.
The book is set in Eiko (Caio Kondo) and Agrandir (Alex Slobzheninov).

Printed and bound by Coach House Printing.

487 King St. W.
Kingston, ON
K7L 2X7
www.brickbooks.ca

Though much of the work of Brick Books takes place on the ancestral lands of the Anishinaabeg, Haudenosaunee, Huron-Wendat, and Mississaugas of the Credit peoples, our editors, authors, and readers from many backgrounds are situated from coast to coast to coast in Canada on the traditional and unceded territories of over six hundred nations who have cared for Turtle Island from time immemorial. While living and working on these lands, we are committed to hearing and returning the rightful imaginative space to the poetries, songs, and stories that have been untold, under-told, wrongly told, and suppressed through colonization.

I don't know how to dream but I'm dreaming.

ALICE NOTLEY

water is like other forms of energy. it transforms.
it does not disappear.

ALEXIS PAULINE GUMBS

Souls take pleasure in becoming moist.

HERACLITUS

CONTENTS

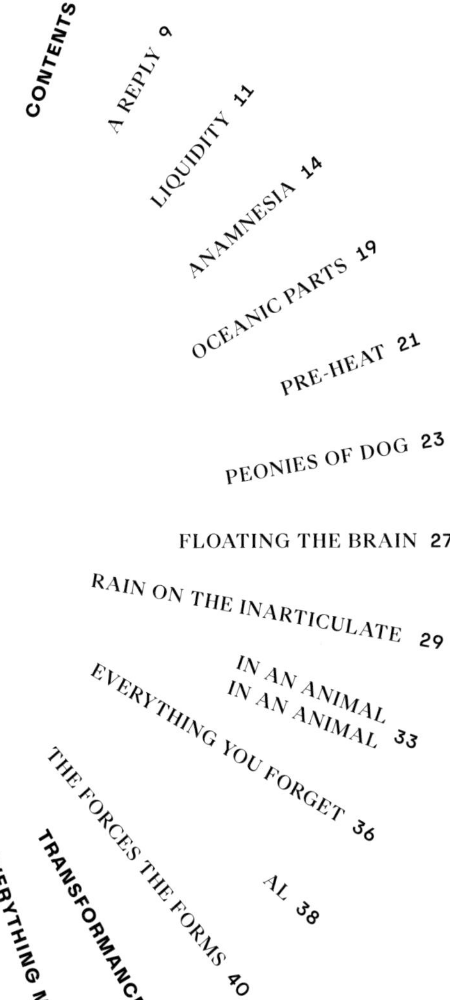

A REPLY

I laid my ear on the ground
my ear on the ceiling
my ear on your voice I could no longer hear
I heard it, and I lay

my whole ear, the full weight
of that radiating organ upon
the space and slept eerily in those folds
and slept in those eerie folds

The voice I heard spirals, you could
say drills, it moved
the opposite way of direct
along the non-arrow of time
of being a person –
spiralic task
ridiculous task
often very shitty task
of being a person

I wanted to become one

By way of approach
it moves away and returns
away and closer
deep into my brains
leaking outwards across the day –
Let me say this
leakage of brains
say this spillage
of my person, let me say
speaking is a ray

The green milk
of me wove
into a wave of this place
an ear of it

I laid it down

on the topmost layer
of time where this
era is hotly composting

and I dampened it
I dribbled on it
I leaked
I gave it my moistures
I gave it my heat

LIQUIDITY

To iterate a star-cream and divulge these contours to myself

Creature curvature
Rolling muscle zone
Wind wind wind wind

It's the first of spring
I don't care about brains

A nervous system today
Said that for her resistance is itself a tonic
And now I'm back in the reading room
Little gusts of self-pleasure in the head –
There's so much thinking to do
With the throat

It sprawls it drools this ardent tube of
Relations I call myself to get through
The grammar I am to the water I am
Through the weft of a wet blanket
That existence wraps round the shivering
Soul but I was online a mere two hours
And got that howling hole feeling

Down networks nimble
For rancor's many heads
Grief's mutations
There I met a verbal energy cop
There I googled von loxsoma cunninghamii
Saw her lacily exchanging garbage for spirit

In sentience's undulations
In totalizing weather, great
Displacer, big breather
Uncontainer riding
Into the mouth
Of whoever

There I walked a very long throat

At the top of the throat
Was a hole going
Someplace. I asked for a form

And now I'm back in the reading
Room finding afford is a limit
Full of holes. Poetry's money
Flows through those
Here's some gentle magenta wealth
Here's some lube, some food
For the possible

I said to the hole
What do I do. Nobody holds the leash
I just drag it around like a style
In amorphous night-scented anxieties
Doom is such a deadly disease
Everything more than it
Is improbable, osmotic
Everywhere leaking into the air

ANAMNESIA

Unmute my skin the warmth of
no one human

Touching off my smallest
necksense in the evening
everyone

Burns an inner sun emitting
readiness or something

Warms me in the dark from
behind your rays I bask in
skinrise

Radiance of sleep's heat
skin's speech all that

I cannot unfeel here in
lockdown. It's April & as
Prince says sometimes it snows

In April which is true now & pretty
much every April in Montreal I never
think I have enough

Time enough money enough
talent enough night to recline in
the outer space

Of my apartment and apprentice at
last to a lucid dream of touch

As philosophy, touch as the
complete works

I had thought about quitting I
had fantasized the radical
pausing of all this

Killing us more infinitely &
actually in the hot hands of
people posing

As people of the globe, people
with a bunker in New Zealand
just in case, people

With a pre-existing sickness
wherein top health's maintained
sucking the life force

Of others to exist as, they say, a
person in this selfsame night
where there is no illness and

No scarcity but in the heart

My cat is warming my lap & my
lap him. I am writing this on him
as he insists and then complains

His kidneys are slowly going
I feel his spine, his ribs, I write
lightly

As his murmurs exhort me, his
feet more perfect than ether

Interrupting every thought I have
in their presence, wiped out by form
& something

I cannot describe, still I could not
spend the day gazing at these feet
only, though I had

Not had enough. One must use what
one has & time was something
I had, time

Was something rare & precious
once

And now more copious than
green will be once April is over
& I forget about the bare
death these trees now

Lay bare, letting me know it's
not all leafy, not all buds &
blossoms blossoming

Not all the sumptuous shade of
fanning canopies but also that
but not only that but even more

So I keep awaiting this other
thing, this other greener thing

& when it comes it's too

Hot. The womb is a creative organ
not limited to reproduction, when
his kidneys go his feet will die

The trees really are about to blow
& the wall I share with the
famous DJ

Is pulsating as everything else
besides does and will do.
Language

Can help, does it hurt & how
much, but my cat ever stoic his
ribs

Jutting out so far, ribs that once
were so padded I never
knew about them

Doesn't get into it even though
he understands English perfectly
as I discovered

Four years ago & now he's sixteen
so for most of his life I didn't
explain things, things

That would have been easy
enough to tell him, things that
affected his life, out of my own lack

Of language between people such
as us. We always know more than
we can say and are

Understood beyond our saying
if we begin by saying

as far

as we can

OCEANIC PARTS

Why do we forget so much when we're alive

Some but not all of it

Full creatures missing

Now our body is reconfigured

Three waves in the bed

Part of me is all muteness that fantasizes speech

There are no parts Michael said

What is it to be departed if there are no parts

If in death the parting is something like an absorption

A release from compartments

Although now that sounds too ideal

Bodies are how I came to love with specificity

Bodies are the parts of speech

The speech is the ocean

The ocean has no parts I think that's what Michael

Meant something like

How a wave is just ocean

Moving through as ocean as oceanic tendency to move

Or how butchers have those ghoulish posters

The shank or the tender parts or the stewing parts but

When bodies separate they can remain in resonance

As Peter van Wyck described in a book I was reading yesterday

Like the sympathetic magic where things once in contact remain

connected, somehow, when they are apart

Your vibratory understanding lent me your loom

You lived without speech as lustrous articulation

As in death you left me the infinite new

End of time new moon new signal new nights

PRE-HEAT

It's 34° C

I swear my fat is melting
And the whole city has a fever
Why do I persist in the wearing
Of clothes in lockdown after three
Months finally just writing naked
In a breeze so very conversant

My cat has been barfing
Almost every day I'm blurbing
A book as they say and late
On the extension, busy melting
My mind feels more than thinks
Lower the motherfucking anchor
And down-channel this violet phase shift

What I desire is to be plumbing
For poetry in any form
Whose form is the school
And if I become
What some part of me is –
There are no parts, I want to
Be copious and sometimes don't
Know how to start anywhere

To desire this character
Flaw that I am, never
Between one life and another
Schrödinger catlike the feral
Inconvenience of poetry
I can't find can't deliver
And there is no system

No system. Sweating
And weeping are forms
Of precipitation for the
Dryness of predictable
Sorrow! And sorrow is wet
To wet the drymouth of
Soul sickness fed on
Industrial-scale evil

Which is how I found myself here
In weather that wants to cook me
And you and probably doesn't want
To cook anyone but even weather
Goes berserk in the vastly

Small imagination necrocapitalism
Dreams of including everyone in
An architecture actively being
Dismantled in the crystal bog
Of imperfect understanding
Around which grow patches

Of self-heal also known as slough
Heal, woundwort, heal-all, all-heal
Small purple flowers with a mouth
A bitter invasive healing
Power for the heart, the mouth
The lymph for moving anger

PEONIES OF DOG

I was in the underworld
Down in my guts
Forgetting my question

Forgetting the courage it takes
Or the looseness, the leisure
And exhaustion it takes to make

Art. In that imbroglio I really
Did think there was a way
To lose somewhere

In my guts, everything
Inside me, semifossorial slow
Worm, status of least concern

A. fragilis so called for the ability
To detach their tail in someone's
Jaws, is this fragilis or totally

Genius, to give half your body
Away to whoever wants it
And keep the rest

Hidden. I wanted to transform myself
Without doing that again, without the
Embarrassment, the expense of my body

Hello, I said. Tell me about nothing.
But as Rilke said there really is no place
That does not see you, and a place

Is always telling you right where you
Are & you might not like it. When I
Got here a week ago, the death-thriven

Forest and the lake
That would not stop talking
Got inside and thought its thoughts

In my mind in a way that
Messed me. What am I
Water's bitch? But kind of I am

And wind is psychoactive
And skin is continuous
Drinking thought through my feet

Dreaming up from where there's no
Seal, there is movement, there is
Your tail again. Dancing's when

You meet your bits in whatever state
And stay with them across the room
Until you're what you are again

And would I know my body
Without the weight of empire
Everywhere upon it, thinking it was

My idea to stay alive and 23 forever
That old chestnut of what's yours
And what's mine, don't let me be dualism's

Stooge, that old shit sandwich without even
The second slice, open-face served
Yes and eaten as if it were

Just what people eat
As if sustenance were self-made
Like shitting your own dinner

In a very neat loop, as the neoliberal tale
Goes, though we know, in every part of us
We know the shit doesn't go back

In, it's for some
Wider loam than
Taxonomic thought can patrol

Self-sustaining never
Needing nobody nonhuman
What is the magic food of self-

Sufficiency? And shit is food
In economy wide and kinky
When you follow where generosity goes

Up the extravagance of death's
Exhaling what you exactly need
Again, alchemically wed

To the light eating
Oxygen out, CO_2 drinking
Ones making shade

Out of heat, green of fire, peaches
Of shit, speech out of wind
Peonies of dog

FLOATING THE BRAIN

In the kitchen worrying about money
Again, water drinks me, water thinks
Me, breath extends me

Through big hydrologics to the bottom
Of the ocean through everyone to begin
Being food, being drink again

Along a long river bottom
Where once many times
We'd been part of us

This life after before a long ceremony
So long it's hard to unremember
To feel at home

In the middle of a city in the middle of a river
My brain floating in juice it produces
Itself

I jiggle a little in the juice it produces to move in
Pleasurabilities, especially in the left lobe
I don't know what the left lobe does

But when I do this it opens and something comes out

Of the brain I perceive with selfsame injured brain
That tries to help her inhabit the damage
How to mindfuck itself by myself

The osteopath says to picture my brain like a jellyfish
Suspended, pulsating, the tentacles fanning
Down as the nervous system feeling itself

The creature is in the connect
So your whole body's the brain
Of the fingering mind, oral arms

Then the waves keep coming
To crash the present most of the world's
Water is in the ocean slowly being moved

As a body of vapour returned as rain as transpiration as thought

RAIN ON THE INARTICULATE

In the dream my eyes emitted a fluid
That was a fractal of the sea cried to scale

In a liquidity lent everywhere, a sea folded
In and leaked in return, perspired by way of

Turning round, as hydrology's juice, as galactic
Pigment, as a tear is the totality of oceanic

Feeling. The eye the organ most limited to surfaces
Has another sense which emits a liquid exigence

Which seeps or wraps to see inside this replete
Wreck of a planet's liquidity moving solutions

From clouds through eyes into dissolving commons
Of wet intelligence melting like ice, as ice

In this rain on the inarticulate, as Eliot almost said
To soften the shabby equipment, swell it, warp it

Rot it, make it sprout. Rain rain rain on language
Surfaces from water's warpings, dampened thought

Intimate office of bodily mixology wrapped
In a fabric of dissolving sutures, soluble memory

To speak of water's entanglements is to dissolve
All lineation. Relation is osmotic, cosmic, contagious

In a talk qʷn̓qʷin̓x̌n̓ describes a century
Of toxic slag in her traditional territory

Dumped by Teck smelter into the Columbia
River before the Colville Tribes took them to court

For 20 years, and in this fight having to prove
Water flows downriver.[6] A droplet of the state

Of colonial decrepitude, stupitude
Flowing through time as a conceptual toxin

Crumbling like the brain cells of a losing reality
In a world infinitely downriver does not stop

Does not stop lead and mercury does not stop
These logics even as they crumble the ocean

Into sediments dredged from 1492, from 1715
From 1965, 2022. Water is the transportation

System of all thought. Between us, through us, through
Space and time. Like a ferry that is the water itself

Up hydrology's workings we rose
Or sank, lugubrious

Or levain, in flesh's sodden opulence
Appearing as a solid, then a vapour

Cream is fur in another form
The sky carried everything that could be

Thought inside of it like spores
That only water could water into possible

Palpable nameable flameable form
Or liquid lived as this condition

Of minglement, before or during
400 years of a dry dream

Of discrete, of leakproof as
A concept that invented plastic and

Metallurgic slag and glyphosate
Since skin doesn't breathe since

It's sealed as an airtight nightmare
Of singular dosage, you eat yourself

Since to remove or dam or constrict or
Deprive or bleed off or siphon or drown

Or understate or sell or pump full of
The only nonhydrophilic substance

Which is oil, would be leachant of
The wet mind of reality

Fouled and filtered by clouds mixed
Into thought, I grow whet & planetary

As a creature
Whose organs clean the water

On a Monday as perpetual liquid vastness
Passes through borders of continuous peristalsis

IN AN ANIMAL IN AN ANIMAL

I was cursed to love the world forever
And especially now sweating it

Out, spitting it out, drinking it in
Before my heart becomes unbeatable

A friend who's not afraid of death
Says deathfear is used as the ultimate lever

To make people do almost anything.
I am afraid of death the way I'm hesitant

Before heroic psychotropic doses, forgetting
What feet are what names what faces are for

I like these forms though there must be
So much more in the universe

That in the afterlife I'll be like one of the mindblown
Who took so much acid they never came down

Hungover in the MRI tunnel I prepare myself
For this, or for losing my mind while living in it

Which to me sounds worse than death. I like my sanity
Too much, and this planet

And I said to my friend okay but
If dying is no problem, don't souls still need a liveable

Place to come be fleshy. His premise being the problem
Of dying is solved in returning, and he would know –

So I guess we'll all be tardigrades, jellyfish, echidnas
and billionaires, which sounds like a plan to me

This is the kind of knowing that got me a B-minus
In Philosophy of Religion class

Before I learned the ways of the academe
And shut up, or said it in a certain way

You know the way & then exhausted
Return myself from forcible forms and travel

Into my own mouth & labyrinthal
Guts, the multiheaded situation

Of me with no demands but that I be planet
To numerosity and receive their dews

Which let me live, which let them
And we live

Out this vast body by the grace
Of subvisible evolving geniuses. I know

About being a body from a body
Through a body because a body in a bigger

Body that needs to go on so I can be your
World, trashing

And filled with trash I didn't ask for
There is a toxin that just keeps travelling

The shrew of all moods is curiosity
I secrete in my guts when I'm shut in

By reason, which is somehow the auspice
For melting & burning the world

And this is why we have to be witches
Ending the empire that feeds on forgetting

To end. A theory afraid of plants
Songs, darkness, wind, water, dreams

And a caterpillar hanging on a thread
From her ass

Who all know
How to end

Not-dying is the apocalypse
Just ahead of being cooked

In wine
Curative for forgetting. When it ends

The world goes on
Transforming, generous in ends

EVERYTHING YOU FORGET

I keep needing to move
Because my mind needs positions for juices

To go there thoughts
Change depending on the angle

Of the mind which is the shoulder too and the light
Draping thought over all of us

My heart has to
Grow because it has to

Because my mother is forgetting
- The spelling of the word *the*

- The names of many vegetables and their uses the ability
- To read as a Gemini and natural genius

I found her frying a cucumber which confirmed for me
Innovation will always be her reflex and

Forgetting is key to innovation one cannot
Rely on standard tellings most of them

Lies and the mind forgets the water
Of the body does not

Navigation by mouthfeel
Through evil you really couldn't make up

In your wildest corporate stupor
Or most inspired thoughtlessness

It's like my mother is stoned
Finding pictures in the water patterns in the sky oh

Everything you forget
inserts love into the silent money said Lisa[💧]

Years ago and now it starts to register
The geographic sadness of my grandmothers in me

And to try and talk about it
Is like squeezing rocks the work the world

Does all day forever
My self-consciousness an alibi

For self-unconsciousness I'm already free
As in I have no value

In dollars. What grows here is form
Of desire astonishing into newforms

Thoughtforms artforms rumpledforms
Feeling into forms' desiring

The yet of
Actual poetry the geo game of leaves sun of fire

Mercury goes direct on flesh
A little fire on my desk

On the election of flesh by flesh for this
Mesh we're in

AL

I must be everywhere

Craving this exact life

To sit with thee, tree

In the lyric song stress, the incompletable weirding

I had no questions only the full-bodied ceremony of falling

Nonexistence is the infinite body

Disappeared as a seed

In the soil of the visible, strokeable

New, new nothing

Dancing up heat in the freezing kitchen

Jumping to stay warm, my thermal suit

Switches on for the radiance

You make in your cells by the effort

Only you do exude as heat

In your conversions

Only you do

Small roving sun

Burning yourself, basking in yourself

Is your primary condition

Of sustenance, vibratory fixing nothing heals

Me, and the missing parts of my body

That you are

Must be everywhere

THE FORCES THE FORMS

This form of life eats beauty
Eats beauty to survive

Beauty its fuel, trashed beauty
At all costs is the economy

But you actually can't kill beauty
So the economy is very unstable

So beauty, but beauty will
Eat the economy

Beauty will unmake
Computers and the shame

Shapes we made tending
Them. Love will eat our brains

When we're tired
Of not checking the source

World without brains
World without checking the source

Of the world
Without checking the source of the forces the forms

What else aren't we knowing
If we don't know

How to make beauty again
How to unstitch ourselves

How to face ongoing violence
That is this form of life, as gentle

As mundane of heart to say
Not even babies, not even you

Who loves beauty. Self-interest is
Apparently the great motivator

And where is the self-interest

Where is the breathing
Self-interest could be

Not wanting to burn in your own bed right
So soaking the pillows & mattress in a nerve gas

To basically burn in your bed a whole new way
In this system that doesn't love anyone[💧]

Not even babies in their sleep to know
This as the world

But they still know it isn't, we do know
In every part of us we know

The way the chemical companies
Protect us

Also the way the sun comes into our room
To shine on this provincial experiment

In power. How can we know
What we know?

The dress on that goddess is hideous
And night & day we sewed & stitched it

Even after the gown of fire melts the town
Even when the gown of wind shreds the house

Way after we knew when the pattern said
Gown it was a shroud we were making

And making. This realism is killing us
Realism carpeting over the shimmering

We are when we destroy
A shabbiness posing as the world

And work for the boss of beauty

TRANSFORMANCES

"Now, bid chaos welcome. It requires a committee, all translators. Undone is not not done."
—Lyn Hejinian

TRANSFORMANCE 1

Thinking is my fighting
said Virginia Woolf in the middle
of war. Are we in the middle of war

A war with the sea, a war with
the air. Who will wear what
the world wore

Lucid and wetly speaking
There's no war you idiots
learn the language

Thinking is how to do it, but it's
not. There is always a war
& this isn't it. This is the floor

And the door and the roof
of the war, and the peace
No knowledge can agree
to eviscerate the sea &

Weaponize the air, winds
of mass destruction blow
the mind wind wind wind

TRANSFORMANCE 2

If the world is a language, if you forget time
to express lavish patterns, another kind of
time. In dandelion season my solar plexus

flexes. Dystopic novels are so tiresome
cuz we already live there. Our way of life
threatens our way of life so you have to see

the enclosure that you cannot see to leave it.
You cannot see it except everywhere in all
directions, on everyone's faces. Their silky

ankles entirely coated. To leave it you cannot.
You begin to notice you cannot. And this
begins your leaving of it?

TRANSFORMANCE 3

In peony season my head explodes quietly, a relief.
Soft eruption visiting everyone or everyone will die
of themselves. I'm a mineral exchanged among the

gentians, a writher, a loaner. Speaking creates
waves that bounce off the structures invisibly ruling.
I echolocate myself and find an evil architecture in

all directions. I keep speaking to know its shape to
not turn into it, to be absorbed. And yes I do receive
these shipments of garbage that aren't 'mine' because

as Eliza suggested, some are psychic and some just
feel with no respect for borders, like the air and like
the water, and also like the fire and its smoke and also

the mountains emanating from, likewise the deer who
as you can imagine are getting out of there and likewise
those for whom the fantasy of border is not an option.

TRANSFORMANCE 4

What if the fragility of the system is actually
the strength of the system?[◊] In wild carrot
intervals I dreamt exhaustingly. Didn't

want to go in the water so I didn't. I began to
walk home along the road. The people driving
by did not know it is customary to transport a

person headed the same way, so they didn't.
My commute passed an empty lot where
I collected a tincture of wild lettuce whose

protection that day seemed the best of what
money could never comprehend. I like poetry
and secretly think everyone does, or would.

The visual is one measure for this and the mind
in its extensions another. I went under a cedar
in the yard and read a chapter of *Through Vegetal*

Being by Luce Irigaray called Losing Oneself and
Asking Nature for Help Again. I was supposed to
go then to a party, so I didn't, opting instead to read

the next chapter, Risking to Go Back Among
Humans, which I did not do, beneath the long
low arms on a towel in the evening.

TRANSFORMANCE 5

This morning in bed I read that in order
to keep step with the climate as it gets
hotter we would have to walk north 10

metres a day. And that afternoon Sachia
said in the red cedars, in 10 years these
won't grow here anymore. The woods

are walking, and dying and surviving.
The owl of knowing so oft flayed by
predation even raptors think is gaga.

Creature feast for hands, hands for
the feast that eats us. My pet predator
calls to me and I produce the chicken

burgers in the freezer for the body of my
familiar in his fur which I then sweep and
roll to hold back the tide of our dispersion

TRANSFORMANCE 6

The sky accumulated. The sun also burrowed.
In the season of long cosmos, some converted
their loneliness, some sizzled in it. Some fantasized

about being left alone. Some forgave their heart
for what their heart wanted. I was these. I was filled
with birds. I was standing in line. I was ancient. I was

enmeshed problems treated topically, singly. At some
point I didn't need a better view, I needed an enema
of politics. We could elect the climate to power

since it already is. In power in power in power
in power. Glorious ostentatious change slow subtle
transformation. Now I'm home drinking wine at my

computer which I shall miss when I'm dead. In late
tansy flush, here is what I'm drinking and saying, here
is the score:

TRANSFORMANCE 7

– Smoke some poison
– Exhale as medicine

– Walk around
– Smoke

– Walk
– Through smoke

– Spinal wave
– Never arrive

– Change position
– Change position
– Change poison

EVERYTHING MINDS[◊]

"the drought
is in the mind
and on the ground"
—Etel Adnan

NEARNESS

Start being a spell
In this sense connected, fragmented as
Points we can't see
In this a storm
That's gathering

Energy
This brain I'm in's alluvium
Misunderstanding what
Is ourselves
Am I – a lady? A storm or

Outright glamour of the sun
Notating endangered radiances
Not a tree nor a bush
I utter my statement
In the lost shape of a choice

It resembles dancing
To look from many angles –
Or whole storm of self, a bachelor
In this enormous connect
How basic is magic

A cloud, a crowd
A cow, a crow, a ripple –
Is everything rhythm?
Chaos & order will keep
Excreting

Lapidary games of thought
That are no game
& no gain so reality
Continues, as lifeforce
As weeds

Reply up cement
My right heart is tight
Solar plexus shock
Help me yellow dock
Illumine pelvic root

Right through my brain
& across existence
The future is peristaltic
Intercourse with
Weather

SMOKE FROM 551 FIRES

The sky had been getting theoretical

Burning mountains

Smoke is different than fog. Less
oxygen
strange headache

burning islands burning horses burning
firs burning

hard to

~~think in~~ Lot of carbonic sky noise
in my eyes

The greyish sky about a foot above
my strange headache
moving

over the land

birds burning spruce burning cedar burning

Esther said it was the trees communicating –

Moisten !

houses burning duff burning cars burning moss burning
eyes

Why are you crying. Why are you crying

I did mushrooms on the weekend
and came to know

subtle bodies

vying for dominance
in the very air

No one is exempt I think, in any realm

from fire
from wetness

So we must work across realms

and poetry will be how. Oh?

As a willful, active and productive use of our organs ◊

Firs love fire. ~~Anyway I can't~~

~~tell what people love~~

but people love getting

moist with their lovers

as a form of travel

So we need midsts

mists

and time

when there is no more time

I DON'T BELIEVE WE CAN SAVE OUR CIVILIZATION; I DO, I DO BELIEVE IT[💧]

In vibratory consequence to the sea

I fall into the dimensions of an hour

The orcas are 'done' Karen told me last night over dinner

On oceanic anoxic tide of unfulfolded brain sadness

Done to in space encircle the earth in loops as lived undulations done

bodies singing voluminous extensions into the sawn-off oceans done

breathing out the tops of their heads

Along the same path the soul blasts at death, out the top of your head

sphincter through which eject spumes of feral joy, or fear breaths

for nearness to be whales / must be

And we'll continue? Bleaching our wealth, our fame?

At Noba's last night, in her partly built house with a feverish child

she said, time is a school. She said, you can use that

Earlier she said there's this thing I always forget to do –

which is breathe in through the top of my head

and exhale out my chest, filling the room not only

but also

CAN YOU TAKE SOMETHING OUT OF THIS WORLD, YES OR NO

Rupert is pruning the roses. Yes.

Poetry is access to information. Yes.

Is a rose an archive, no
A memory, yes
of silky sense, yes
A garment? No
Many garments, yes

Yes fresh
the dress
of the mind so
I know I know I know

I court a form yes
Windward
on the processual
rosebuds, yes

Or no, how I came
to yes in the arboretum
of epistolary flowers
and eat this raindrop & speak
with the glossy vocal yes
powers, the bird yells of
power, the rotations of
softness, all this

I remember
happening, yes coming to
pass away a spell, to be
come glossy, yes and furred
touting instruments yes
of not-death nor shortage nor no

QUEEN OF HEAVEN

The ecstasy of communication
I haven't been having, and Venus
The evening star, Queen of Heaven
Is "dry as a bone" David Harry

Grinspoon says in *Venus Revealed*
Of footage taken inside her "thick and opaque"
Privacy, the Baltis Vallis snaking over southern
Plains, passing massive arachnoids, petal-type volcanoes

In the Delta of Venus winding through plains south of Ishtar
Terra to Atla Regio where bloom lava flowers 100 miles
Wide. Venus is similar in size and composition to Earth
And may once have been more temperate & more lovely

When those Vallis flowed, and flowers not of
Lava but fecundity's openings opened before
Becoming so hostile, the weather permanently
Overcast with sulphuric acid and 500 degrees

Another way Venus is similar to Earth is
She has about the same amount of carbon as we do
All of it in the atmosphere, cooking once and future
Mere creatures. If we also put all our carbon in the air

We too would cook beyond all life and death.
Time is strange there, a day is longer than a year
And that makes sense to me. What if the body
– What if!!? is a slower flower, rotating the opposite

Way to everything Law while being cooked on Earth
More slowly. As the morning star is the evening star
We were warned by the goddess of love & war & rain
& storms to keep it in the ground of the bend of the world

ANEMONE

Eye of the sea
portals, orifices

mouths that see
turquoise anus flowering

gives birth through
the mouth

of the sea

This is the situation –
This is the situation –

Esther says it's not that the climate depends on what we do or don't do –
it's that we depend entirely on clouds

to travel into reality with
to think

with anemones, lavishly
and without money

through cracks in existence
named Bezos Gates Buffett Arnault Ortego Slim Zuckerberg Walton Koch Bloomberg

who offer such drab death
to everyone

Will you buy this water, this air, this chemo
Will you accept manmade apocalypse with no men to answer
to cosmic generosity –

or pleasure from the sun
while pleasuring the moon?

NONPLANET IRRATIONAL BARREN MOON

They said you were geologically dead
and they would say that about who

makes the seeds cream, the oceans move
in me, whose calendar revolves

whose calendar of absence
whose calendar is change

who walks me home
O moon make me less blurry!

Make me a detailed plan through
swarms of death beside and below

travelling this edible sprawling body
through abyssal fractals leaning

back to my origin's origin, continuing
in the deep element to find my mind

by flap and by shimmer, onward toward
I do not know – into the deep curtain, the vast I

sometimes stupidly certain I am totally lost
or have never been. It makes me happy just to try to describe

the delicate green landings of the pine
flying in a hectic jagged way

I would spend all my money
admiring your language

in moonbaked sheets
the small blue, the oily black

woad when I first saw you
and my concepts went driving slowly away

into a different muscle group entirely
like upside down against a wall

taking in your light, transforming it
in my body – pressure, succession, heat

How to say it straight
what turns around

into a swan, a pulse
leaking all over the floor

dissolving in it   O moon

The wound gets healed
The wound gets healed

O moon !

CRADLE OF ZOOM

I listen to my reluctance, curious to see how far it goes
But you are an artist, the person said
A person with high hopes for art
I had high hopes for art too and felt that the motion
Of art was first a kind of training
To simply not be sick in the chaos
And not swallow the sick back down
A physical training for withstanding evil
I found that I wanted to bite, to be soft, to ride & send messages
I seem to require these tensions
There's nothing formless
But the terror of speaking on a zoom call
Has a whole new motion new quease
We were being asked to accept this, to acclimate
To a realm replacement merely
These imperfect momentums are empty
The content is your art
Not as *objet* but as your extreme training whereby you can make anything
Strange, this is the least obvious one
Jung said the body is the densest part of the unconscious
My density started to float and dissolve after zooming
The fast-moving money of aliveness strangest of all

When I finally left my house

I found that I wanted to hide, and that I actually could

In the axiology of plants and their care I mean weeds I mean

I have 30 seconds left and must tell you my desk has an eye

It's been here all along

In the grain of the wood, I failed to mention

How it cares for me, but now that we're here I don't want to omit

The details the sorcery the plainness it takes

For things to appear

WEDNESDAY

Sandra and I meet to celebrate
my not getting the scholarship
She advises me on how to develop
my fire body

Poetry finds money in the air

The Anthropocene names the epoch
of the giantest narcissism
in geologic time

It's not surprising that such narcissism
might be a death wish but Jeff

Poetry means learning to deal with yourself

And when sadness overtakes me, my inner husband
sings for me

My elbow on cool stone, the ocean in its boneless rolling, the enrobing air –

Elsewhere, my body had a completely different function

ANGELS

The angels work
At night, sitting on the face

Of efflorescence with their hairy
Bods to give plants wings

Angels, with their pincers, their many arms
& wings, tireless to blur the blossoms

Moth are you the angel, bedecked in eyes
Monstrous tongue, lashing & insisting

They left their "wallet at home"
They are "getting paid next week"
They "have been changing"
They are "not tired"
Do they "know Anni Albers"
They taught her "everything"
They had a "meltdown"
And it was "the best thing that could have happened"
Though it felt "terrible, a living death"
And sometimes you just "need to die"
For a "while, in a little bag" spun
From your ass, and "melt yourself down"
To find your "form," your body's new
Grammar
I mean
I dreamt this pattern
In the total darkness
Of my ass-spun sack
And "this is totally normal" and

"Much harder" if you "fight" it
Being "so attached to forms"
Even "wormforms" –

It's a lot of "work" and to
Fuck the flowers all night helps
Alleviate something
They say, in their iridescent
Way, it's a strange
Imagination the people
Dwell in though
As if the floral
Was normal and nothing
To "get excited about"
Preferring everbearing
Wastelands, steroidal
Abundance from a button
Pressed, all things come
For which they pay and pay
Out their lithosphere, hydrosphere
Biosphere, atmosphere
Cryosphere, noosphere
And then worry about it

It's sweet in a way and very
Abnormal on the earth
And that's saying a lot
When at this point every
Flowerfucking angel
Is what they really
Need

KITCHEN DANCEPARTY

In the animate way the space came to show us

The space came to greet us, space showered down on us

The space elaborated us space elected us

The space said fill me with your mind of gesture space

Goaded us the dark sky above us

Where we moved space was more space

And it opened for us

The year was just beginning and already

We'd remembered how to make our own heat how to make anything in the air

How to have bodies how to think with our fingers & our hair

How to receive space, how to thank the dark
Space offering how to move the air how to rattle
The room how to flame how to motion
How to surge how to dreambody how to pray how to feel us how to go
Forever for however long how to travel how to power how to
Love existence how to respond to the glamour of night
How to think with our hips how time unspools from us
How we pattern existence how we drink from the cup of newness
nowness & night

WET DREAM

"So drenched that night we all were from tough knowledge
Spilling out across the dark earth
In this vulnerable, pulsing mother field."
—Joy Harjo

MYRTLE

De-doctored cure round deep
Is a phrase you wrote me
You're who I want to be with if I
Sever my femoral artery, or if I wed
We still need to finish *The Secret Life*
Of Plants which was interrupted
By falling in love with your body
I was already in love with everything
Else, as once in the night I told you
I wanted to marry, not as innovation
But because it felt like we already were
And when we broke up you sent me
Pictures of heavily feathered angels
In the Hagia Sophia
I needed fuckloads of feathers
To stay afloat and who could I ask
But you, and when we broke up
I felt the literalness of the term –
A signal breaking up
Anne Carson says beauty spins and the mind moves
Or I suspend in your mind as a child
At the time we thought little of it

And I thought love would be very
Clear and mysterious like a strange eye
That would see into and admit like
A sphincter into the flower in the heart
And was not wrong
But I didn't know I could care so much about
The new shelves you've built in your room
And when we got back together I thought
I saw a Catasetum eject pollen-masses &
A Mormodes twist its column, as Darwin put it
But I never imagined I would be invited to compost
My whole heart for someone only to meet again, admittedly refreshed
Or that one could order gallons of honey in the mail
Which turns me on as do
Your texts of sea caves and giant hogs
Playing chess wearing dozens of avocadoes
It's really the only way I could love
Though I suppose there must be other ways
De-doctored cure round deep
Into the spiral at some point and before then
Love is one of the strangest things that can happen
From being the other of the same, freed to finally be

the other of the other[◊] to remind me how

All this explains nothing next to all this touch

OTHER ECONOMIES

A portal is open and things flow in
and out or they stop flowing

Less about content and more this flow
of content – is our aphrodisiac

Today I read about how corals spawn –
once a year, after the first full moon

of summer, reefs pulse in pink weathers
of jellies, spurts, spumes, a blizzard

of group sex. To be greens like hotpinks
erotic purples lined with shouting yellow nipples

secreting sperm'n'eggs in solitary splendour
for 900 years a violet brain flocked with green

leather entrypoints pulsating tentacles of red
violescent sea whips eating brain eggs or

tongues with fingers fingering flower animals
of feel, branching into buoyant pleasure gardens

who bring the creature out of the hole. They
can also asexually bud, anytime

While I sit at my desk in my apartmenthole
reading Suely Rolnik who says *Art is thus*

an ecological reserve for the invisible species
that populate our animal body in its generous

germinative life; a wellspring of courage
for confronting the tragic. The moods of waves

The medicines of hole-dwelling. Lives we haven't
yet met in our very large selves as we dissolve

POWER

Power. I slipped it off
And moved quietly

Around a cloud
Of hot inequities forming, 12, 13

14 – I understood
Some people are hot for it

But not me. It was easy to say
You take it –

My jagged flame
My splendid rage

Such was my protest and my experiment
Adolescent intuition is so hardcore, close to god

Deathless, holes through flesh
Numinous feels by any means

Too bad you can't get away from power.
Power.

It did not interest me
I didn't know what to call the thing

I sought. Last night I dreamt I finally
Went to a dentist

Who took my money without
Cleaning my teeth, alluding to serious problems

For which I'd have to return.
Teeth in dreams

Are famously about power. I went
To see a man about cleaning mine

Who didn't so I would have to return.
What kind of power did I think was power

The shady dentist
Avatar for abuse of power makes me laugh

He seems so counterfeit. But how much
Counterfeit power passes?

My adolescent solution to remove
The problem of power in the world

By pulling out all my teeth was
Just what dentists in their wolf-dentures

Extracted from wolves
Raised in hideous teeth factories

Wanted. It took me around 20 years
Suffering over love, suffering over art, suffering

To please everyone, suffering
From broke-ness, suffering

At abuses of power to see that power
Is not the problem

LET US HELP THE HYDRA CLEAR AWAY THE FOG◊

Trying to understand the distinction
Between form and material

(Fog will be helpful)

For example a party
You enter, as materials

As fog form-filled with speech
For instance in 2012 the arctic

Was 1/2 ice-free, sipping wine
Into one's beauty so urgently

Filling up form
Your materials speak

Flit or bounce but form
(The arctic) will be

Completely ice-free in
Our lifetime – form opens for you

As hostess, a hydra admitting
An ecstatic zoo or

Form uses you, you're the plume
Not the name, you're currency

You don't need travel and the floors
Were dirty so I cleaned them, this is one

Technique to expel fog
Formed from processual

Time, explaining for example my
Ability to digest plastics or

My repose, this wish to be a garden simply
Falling

Into dialogue with whomsoever flagellates
Visit me here, multivalent

Babysitter of the spangled mind ◊

WET FLAME

Jill says the tongue is the visible tip
Of the brain, and if you hold it still
You can't think

Thinking is movement is the tongue's
Erudition, glitching
In the wet electric brain

Which sounds hazardous
Like listening to the radio
In the bath, yes

It's much like this
Being a body
Being a precarious wet immersion

Balanced on a rim
Of fascination
At risk of death tuning

To the waves
Of others
Alone in the tub

A voice in your ears
A song that comes on
Flooding you

Til the bath gets
Cold & spirals away
You leave footprints

You go downstairs
You don a new dress
You travel through the earth

(SOME SOLUTIONS

A solution to inside/outside
A solution to false metaphysical premises
A solution to rectangle dominance
Is being a body
Who dissolves)

SCALAR

Reality is the most
heartbreaking substance

Ever drunk through every pore
nostril word

Every secret entrance to the
face. Ariana says the instruction is

To love it at all costs.[◊] An
ongoing task

Since the real requires
stupidity, so much stupidity

For whatever reason. This place
is so stupid

And the light loves it, the water
runs it

The soil of it is where we come

To meet each other in whatever
state until we're what we are again

When I lie facedown on the ground
with my arms out

I can carry the whole thing
It's exactly the weight I can

Hold though that seems crazy
This place is crazy

Like that, no one said that it
wasn't

As I hold the whole
fucking rock in my arms

The mismatch in scale is a phase
& I think we can relate anyway

LUBE OF YOUR EYE

If intelligence survives, and it will
If intelligence survives, and it's all that survives
Will the water inside us remind us
Of that time we were a river during
The lube of your eye, the wet of your tongue
During the Columbia River so you can speak
Time, temporarily river vein of the world
To move in as us to become someone else
Evaporating into a pulse of damp thought
That remembers where it's been and what it is –
It is a diving bird, it is a watersnake watching it
All in S-curves of fluid time as rivers at every scale
Makes the motion that evening and concrete & everything
Is, though yesterday did not appear to move at all.
Rivers of air, rearranging particles from here to
Places I have never been. If I breathe
If I breathe them in and send my love
In particles to greet you, whoever you are, if you are
Rhythmically through the thought of the world, entering
Me at different moments, adding, changing change.
If my thought privates and goes on sleeping the sleep
Of lack given to me by fascism in the water, fascism in the air

Will love's liquid moving through tell me if thriving

Survives? If thriving survives, and it will

Will rivers, will veins, will eyes? If I breathe? If I breathe you

Into my mind, would I hear you, if we heard you

Would we understand, is understanding enough

Never is. What will eat us, anything?

Everything?

FERAL PRAYER

I give up. I give up asking. I give up asking for anything
less than billions of gills sporulating revolution's pheromone.
The trash of civilization is who I love. Anything less than
billions of salmon returning themselves to the forest.
All I ask are rivers, predictable flowering seasons, storm
corridors & wet wide will to surge the brilliance we are
omitting in the practice of citizenry to a system who hates
99% of itself. Big black cat of the heavens, purr this numbness
to death. My civilization suppresses weeds as much as women
so weeds grow to the size of the sky & rain down seeds on our
heads so pharma is free, so loneliness undone among monocrops
in eruptions of yellow. The alternative is wind so strong I fear
the trees thrashing at the edge of ability to hold on & flex
losing bits of themselves on the roof like us losers –
colossal loss is us, is the alternative to a pulse of salmon,
a peristalsis of wings. Great undulation of oceans, retilt
brainwaves glitched in place & make intelligence surge
in the stupidest places of this situation of waves, salmon
streams & sky, by way of orgasm & plasma & everything
unfinished, so life stays alive I give up asking for anything
less than this kiss

LANGUAGE OF THE BIRDS

"I was unspeakable so I ran into the language of others."
—Kathy Acker

Bright sentience of morning comes
Out of a concussed cloud –

Hypnotizing on its radiant surface
The mind is a complex formal solitude

For a week in flames
And the panic of being trapped

Inside a skull. A presence that moves through
Distortion, through bodies and through

Big bright mind today, white-throated
Sparrow on chains of utterance rides

Right into the window and dies instantly.
If song is invisible is it perceivable

To those who have dissolved
Into air? Every organism

Produces some kind of signal💧
To move among and according

To voices the living make in bodies
In the intermediate state

Of having bodies – a mouth
Or thighs for rubbing song

Shapes the waves we're in –
Releasement through the ears into glistening

I'm inside your language
Cut with its rhythms, half

Awake, spreading into the alley
Into the air where the mind is spatial

Muteness is a matter of curiosity that first
Returns things, the dawn correspondence

Spatialized arousal, have you seen mine
Thought is a circulatory system

Of which my mind is a node
That speaks the muscularity

Of this, and the colour
Needed a throat to sing

And a throat needed someone &
For some reason it needed me who

Could not really sing, for the air to move
Through is what I mean by song

Then I awoke in my differentiated body
And I had work to resist. I love work

And if sex is as hilarious as you make
It sound I will go looking for it

In the trees, looking in the air of fucking's
Joke around which swims all other things

I came with my vocal sadness
To the bend in the alley

In the raging dawn to dissolve
In the fabric of utterance

Rhythmically looping sound
Through bodily circuitry

To study resonance's helix
Insane with ergonomics I leak into air

To ask you to dissolve something
I may never be able to explain

In these elongations of mind
Into audible time

So I came with my problem to
The dawn, it seemed like the place

Tuesday, presence fields overlap
In waves

Travelling through waves. Sound
Is an apparition I rely on –

Elaborate vocal rolls roll through me
Extend you small bird through

Space. Concentric enunciation
Your soundbody enfolds me –

So are you small or are you all of space?
Intermediary airy flesh I slip into

Your vocal folds, soak my I in plenitude
And when I couldn't speak

You spoke steadily, electric blue, my brain enflamed
Words

Meant very little, foreign, sharp. Speech seeks a border
To eradicate

A sparrow in my throat-
Damped song or regular

Unmarked proclivity for verbal
Pleasure, a rosiness

In your chest enfolds me, the dawn
Vomiting song in rivulets of mouthy

Warpings, genuflections
Rhythmic head

Bird language seams between
Utterance and architecture

In verbal pulses, concentric
Presence. A crease increasing

Older folds is the day appearing
Into the day, is another

In your songbody enfolded
In the day's prism for brains

Speaking is a ray – say it, say
Body's no discrete killable finitude

Where speech goes there you go
On the long tongue of mind

Music extrudes you. Speech-soaked, mutely
Concentric head

Muteness is about grief it seems to me now
A phase of it

That's incoherent, there's another phase where
The clarity

Just cuts. I'm listening to you because you bring
These phases together, or because

You sing through walls you sing on my head
You personage of space, shimmering there

Who I did not not see. Bewildered I wade into
Your utterance erupting, related by air

And time, related by a song, wading through throats
Related

By wind and time (the same wind
Rode)

I've been watching a vine form elaborate decisions
All along

The balcony. Every vibrant need exerts
A force

Its body are decisions. Its body are transportation
I stupidly wept

Writing an email to my dad. I stupidly
Wept

During a zoom reading, too close and too far
Everyone

From my enormous buckling
Face

I is a node in a flickering fabric
Language, long songs, leisure

Move through walls, states
Vestibules, spiked ledges

Trees that elaborate around the
Life so life can go on thinking and

Have a place to hide. The soft vibrations
Of the female *zhouu zhouu zhouu*

While the male has no subtlety
Sch*weeep* sch*weeep*. They like it.

The cats in their predatory
Morning slinking get no relief

I've seen. I worry I'm reinjuring
My brain with this relentlessness

Needing to stop when I can't stop.
But I just think that's true, which is

Part of the injury unrelated to the
Impact. Attempting to 'take a break'

And read something unrelated I try
The Tibetan Book of the Dead which

In the original Tibetan is called *The
Great Liberation by Hearing in the*

Intermediate States. The intermediate
States being: waking, dreaming

Meditation, the time of death
And the two successive phases of the

After-death. A concussion is somewhere
Between all of these

A word is a wave, and a song
Is the weave

The weave is long. A song a long way
A word song way

I remember parties that cured me
A spontaneous wealth

Arising amidst bodies
In regular rooms accelerating

Polyvocal, kinked
A true party was not often

Found in peopled rooms
Those mysticisms of conditions

Marriage of true minds
Sluicing around before

The dawn's language
Of birds enters

Thought thresholds
Seeking audience with the dawn

And the first thing I noticed
Was each morning

Raged so differently
On Friday you bleat

Experimental jokes
This party moves in waves

Of chat through evergreen
An ash that was

Sunday is muted, violet, flowing
Tree to tree, delicate bird work

On sung fabric of space of
Day's opening keeps us

Here querying the air in sapphic
Vocables, so the sun rises

Your speech manifests as Monday
On chains of utterance from a cedar

A neighbour sneezes and vanishes
To the shifting light, parallaxing

The opposite of rock or song
Is liquid rock is goo

Becoming early
In a home distributed

From Guyana to Alaska, all this way just
To shag on the power lines, last year's

Grapevine, the tattered cedar
You really love. Visibility is

The smallest part about you
An envelope for organs

To carry through the air
Speech is the process in which you live

Through walls, through anything solid
To trouble, any border to debunk

Hearing is nearness is open
Feeling

Vesicle of the possible thought
Rearing

Sameness and solitude organize
Revealing

Architectures stolen in maximum
Daylight

Reason resists almost everything
Noteworthy

The mind is drugs
That's the premise of this study

That's the thing, that's the lack
That isn't here, in the air – help

I could ask the birds for
The mind is a sparrow in the grapevine

Carrying a length of plastic sheeting in his beak
A bird, a never-ending nerve

Elongating thought across the sky
Through verbiage into vocal foliage

The mind is a minor power of the
Sun tending an amnesia

As I step into the weather of your
Speaking

Birds are people who travel
The wave inside brain sun –

Shines the meeting is time
Spun from sun –

All of this saying
Is about saying

And if I could
And how I would

And when I did what I
Said was speak to me

Phrases marked with a ◊ in the book are quotations. These and other references are noted in order of appearance.

5 Opening epigraphs:
Alice Notley, *Certain Magical Acts*
Alexis Pauline Gumbs, *Dub: Finding Ceremony*
Heraclitus, *The Complete Fragments,* trans. William Harris

19 "there are no parts," from a conversation with Michael Stone

20 Peter C. van Wyck, *The Highway of the Atom*

23 Rainer Maria Rilke, "Archaic Torso of Apollo," trans. Stephen Mitchell

27 Osteopath Sheryl Hoo shared this image of the brain-nervous system connection as a jellyfish. Moving with my jellyfish profoundly changed my experience of living with/in a post-concussion brain.

29 "rain on the inarticulate" is a reference to TS Eliot's phrase "raid on the inarticulate" in "Burnt Norton"

29 Astrida Neimanis' scholarship on/with water profoundly influenced this poem and many other water-based poems in the book. In particular their essay "Hydrofeminism: Or, on becoming a body of water" and book *Bodies of Water: Posthuman Feminist Phenomenology* have soaked into my thinking and the cosmological fibres of this book.

30 qʷn̓qʷin̓x̌n̓ , Patti Bailey, discussed this case in a keynote she gave at *Overburden: Geology, extraction and metamorphosis in a chaotic age*, Oxygen Art Centre. With gratitude to Patti for her input into the poem. Full talk here: overburden.ca/archives.html

33 Udavi Cruz-Márquez, from a conversation

34 Echidnas can sleep through wildfires to survive them, using a kind of hibernation called torpor.

37 Lisa Robertson, *The Weather*

41 "these systems that don't love any of us, and that turn all of us against ourselves," adrienne maree brown in conversation with Angela Davis, November 18, 2020, UC Davis (online event)

43 Lyn Hejinian, *My Life*

45 Virginia Woolf, "Thoughts on Peace in an Air Raid" (essay): "But there is another way of fighting for freedom without arms; we can fight with the mind."

48 "What if the fragility of the system is actually the strength of the system?" This question arose in an Anarchival schizo-somatic writing session organized by Csenge Kolozsvari and Diego Gil through the Sense Lab at Concordia University, 2018.

48 Luce Irigaray, *Through Vegetal Being* [co-authored with Michael Marder]

53 Joe Sheridan and Roronhiakewen "He Clears the Sky" Dan Longboat, "The Haudenosaunee Imagination and the Ecology of the Sacred"

53 Etel Adnan, *Time*

59 Novalis (Friedrich Hardenberg), fragment 1339. Cited by Giorgio Agamben in *The Man Without Content:* "Novalis's definition of poetry as a 'willful, active, and productive use of our organs'"

60 Alice Notley, *Certain Magical Acts*

61 Sara Hamming, *Choreography on the Face* (performance lecture). My quotation is a variation on the original, which reads, "Can you take something out of this world? / Yes or no?"

63 David Harry Grinspoon, *Venus Revealed: A Look Below the Clouds of Our Mysterious Twin Planet*

64 A bow to all those working to keep fossil fuels in the ground, and to the Fossil Fuel Non-proliferation Treaty: fossilfueltreaty.org

77 Joy Harjo, *Conflict Resolution for Holy Beings*

79 Anne Carson, *Eros the Bittersweet*

80 Letter from Charles Darwin to JD Hooker, 19 June, 1861: "I shall never rest till I see a Catasetum eject pollen-masses, and a Mormodes twist its column."

81 Elizabeth A. Povinelli, *Geontologies: A Requiem to Late Liberalism*. The fuller line reads: "as Luce Irigaray might have said, from being the other of the same, freed to finally be the other of the other."

82 Suely Rolnik, "Lygia Clark and the Art/Clinic Hybrid," trans. Micaela Kramer

86 Stéphane Mallarmé, *Divagations*

87 "deathless Aphrodite of the spangled mind," Sappho, *If Not, Winter: Fragments of Sappho,* trans. Anne Carson

88 Jill Purce, from her Healing Voice workshop: healingvoice.com

91 Ariana Reines, "UT PICTURA POEISIS" (essay)

97 Kathy Acker, *Bodies of Work*

99 Bernie Krause, from an interview we did over email: https://emergencemagazine.org/interview/earwitness-to-place/

ACKNOWLEDGEMENTS

For my mother Siobhan Robinsong, who read to me, and gave me wildness. Everything about this book comes from this, returns to this.

I'm grateful for uncountable strands of friendship, encounter, research, and generosity that coalesced as this book.

Immense gratitude to Sonnet L'Abbé for editorial brilliance, and to Alayna Munce and everyone at Brick Books for bringing *Wet Dream* into the world with prowess and deep care. Flora Wallace, thank you for indigo rivers/veins/terrains of the cover, and Kevin Lo for designing this beautiful object. *Wet Dream* was born in a literal dream where a voice told me in no uncertain terms to send my manuscript to Brick, before I had a manuscript, or any thought of publishing with them. Thank you voice in the dream, whoever you are.

The book grew out of a chapbook with House House Press called *Liquidity* (2020) – huge gratitude to David Bradford and Anahita Jamali Rad for that initiating invitation. Those and other poems in *Wet Dream* have also appeared on BBC Radio 3 on the program "Between the Ears," and in *Effects Journal, o bod, Watch Your Head: Writers and Artists Respond to the Climate Crisis,* and *The Minutes of the Hildegard von Bingen Society for Gardening Companions.*

Financial support from the Canada Council for the Arts and the Conseil des arts et des lettres du Québec was crucial in the writing and research of this book – thank you CCA and CALQ for the privilege of time and space.

I'm grateful to generous and brilliant friends and mentors who read and commented on these poems at many stages: Julie Joosten, David Bradford, angela rawlings, Eliza Robertson, Joni Murphy, Sina Queyras,

Florence Uniacke, Sophie Seita, Orlando Reade, Alfons Raoul, and Merlin Sheldrake.

Shôken Michael Stone, your bodhisattva intelligence is everywhere in these poems. There are no parts. I miss you every day and am grateful for your friendship, in life and death. This book is also for you.

Gratitude to my teachers, formal and not. Astrida Neimanis' thinking on/with water profoundly rearranged my understanding of the world; their ideas watered many of these poems into being. Reading Rilke's *Duino Elegies* and *Inanna: Queen of Heaven and Earth* on zoom with Ariana Reines & Invisible College at the beginning of the pandemic escorted me through that bizarre realm-switch in medicinal & generative ways. Many poems in this book are inspired by conversations at / uncanny resonances with Invisible College in those early days, and still. Lisa Robertson's books and ways of being have accompanied me in writing and thinking and living, as continual teachers. Sina Queyras has been a radical ally and fierce & loving teacher, thank you Sina. Priya Huffman, thank you for teaching me to read the bizarre language of my dreams – their intelligence and your generosity have been deep guides. Huge thanks to the incredible teachers, friends, and colleagues I have had the privilege of thinking with at the Geopoetics Symposium on Cortes Island, and at Concordia University through the interdisciplinary humanities PhD program. The work and generosity of each of these thinkers has altered my cells, my understanding of poetry, my perception of the world, and definitely this book.

To the poets and thinkers whose lines are quoted throughout this book – thank you. Thinking with and from your work has been my ultimate pleasure.

O my friends! Your inspiration, conversation, and love are what this book is made of. Special thanks to Andréa, Sybille, Sarah, Michael, Kaeli, Ilona, Cosmo, and those who appear in the poems for allowing me to include your words and to riff on them – Sandra, Eliza, Michael, Nadia, Udavi, Noba,

Karen, Esther, Sheryl, Ariana, Cosmo, Bernie, the birds of Jeanne Mance, and Merlin.

Beloved family (blood, in-love/in-law, chosen, poet kin; Cortes family, Montreal family, English family, Irish family) thank you for inspiration and support always. I love you so much. Alfons, your silky companionship was my rock (2005–2020), and now from another realm, thank you forever. Merlin Sheldrake, mercurial creature, your mind is everywhere in these poems, this book is also for you ♡

Gratitude to the water that composes us, sustains us, dreams us, and connects us through space and time.

Erin Robinsong is a poet and interdisciplinary artist. She is the author of *Rag Cosmology* (Book*hug, 2017), which won the AM Klein Prize for Poetry, and several chapbooks including *Liquidity* (House House Press, 2020). Her work has appeared on BBC Radio 3, and in journals and anthologies including *o bod, Vallum, The Capilano Review, Effects Journal,* and *Watch Your Head: Writers and Artists Respond to the Climate Crisis*. Collaborative performance works with Andréa de Keijzer and Hanna Sybille Müller include *This ritual is not an accident, Facing away from that which is coming,* and *Polymorphic Microbe Bodies*. Originally from Cortes Island, Erin lives in Tiohtià:ke/Montréal.

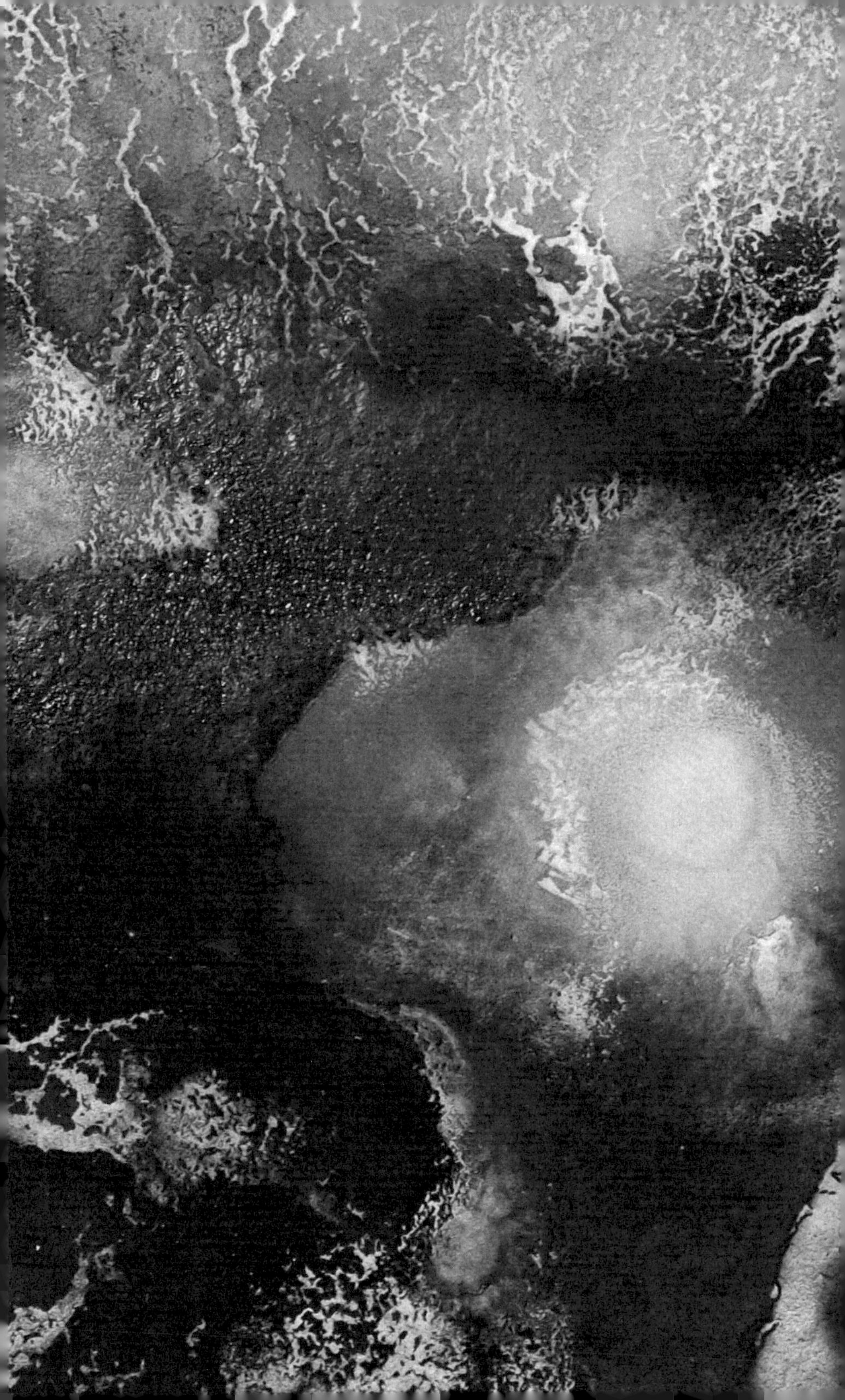

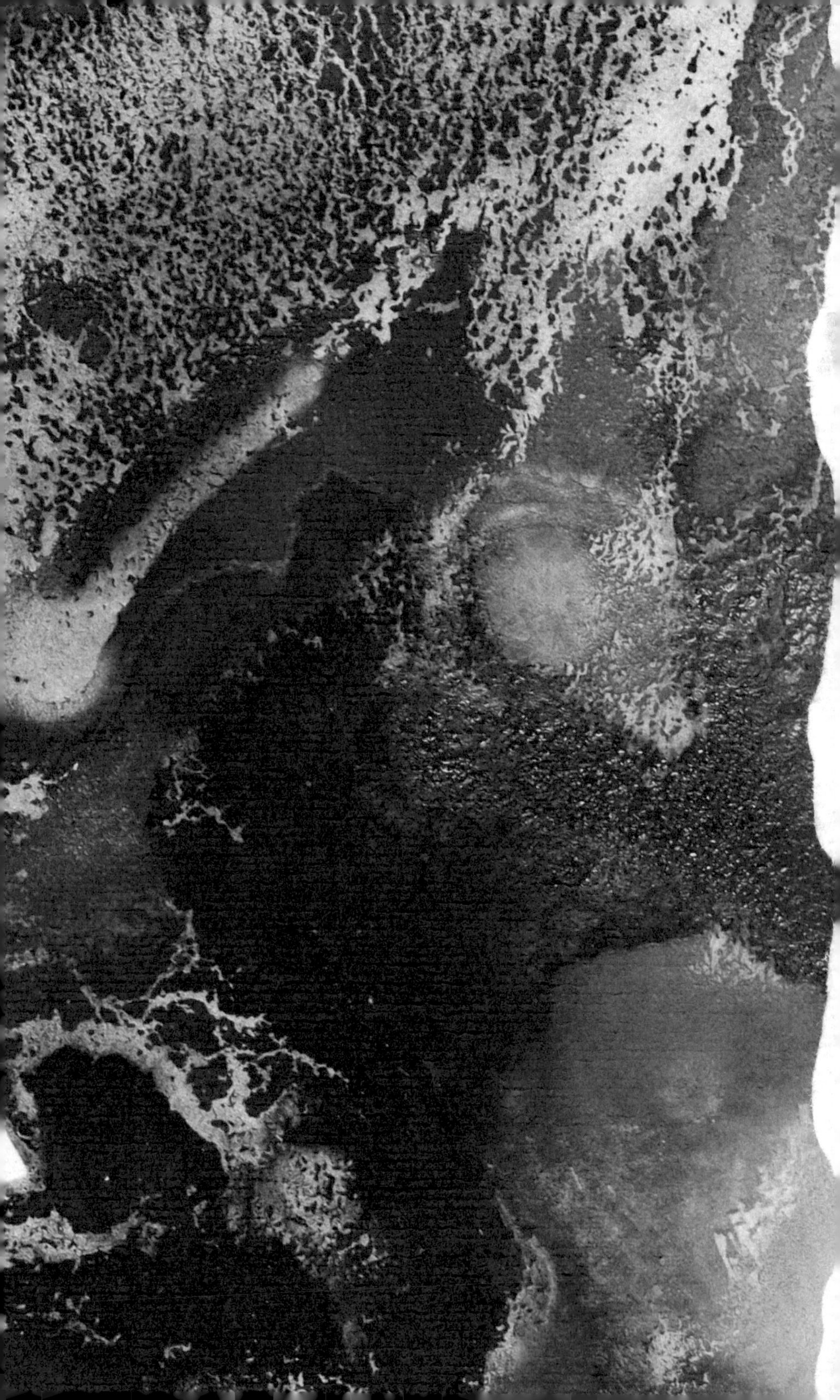